The Stealth Health Meal Prep Cookbook

From Beginner to Advanced: Your Complete Guide to Healthy, Convenient, Delicious and Tasty Meals

MASSIMO BIANCHI

COPYRIGHT

© 2025 MASSIMO BIANCHI All rights reserved. No part of this publication may be reproduced, distributed, or transmitted in any form or by any means, including photocopying, recording, or other electronic or mechanical methods, without the prior written permission of the publisher, except in the case of brief quotations embodied in critical reviews and certain other noncommercial uses permitted by copyright law

DEDICATION

To all the busy individuals who refuse to compromise their health and well-being despite life's relentless demands—this book is for you.

To the parents juggling careers and families, the students navigating tight schedules, and the professionals working tirelessly to achieve their dreams while seeking balance at the dinner table.

To my mentors, who taught me the value of perseverance, and to my loved ones, who've inspired countless recipes shared in these pages.

And finally, to the reader holding this book: may it empower you to nourish your body, simplify your days, and find joy in the kitchen, one meal at a time.

Stealth Health Cookbook

TABLE OF CONTENTS

COPYRIGHT 2
DEDICATION 3
PREFACE 10
INTRODUCTION 12
   What is Stealth Health? 13
   The Basics of Meal Prep 15
PART 1: FOUNDATIONS OF STEALTH HEALTH MEAL PREP 17
CHAPTER 1 18
   The Essentials of Meal Prep 18
      Replacing Refined Ingredients Without Sacrificing Taste 22
      Simple Hacks to Cut Sugar, Salt, and Fat 24
      Mastering Flavor the Healthy Way 25
      Techniques for Making Healthy Food Taste Irresistible 26
PART 2: STEALTHY RECIPES FOR EVERY MEAL 28
CHAPTER 2 29
   Energizing Breakfasts with a Twist 29
Spinach and Banana Pancakes 30
Carrot Cake Muffins 31
Avocado and Berry Smoothie Bowl 32
Sweet Potato Breakfast Hash 33
Zucchini and Chocolate Chip Muffins 34
Cauliflower Breakfast Scramble 35
Pumpkin Spice Overnight Oats 36
Quinoa Breakfast Bowl with Pomegranate and Nuts 37
Sweet Beet and Berry Smoothie 38
Hidden Veggie Breakfast Wraps 39
CHAPTER 3 40

Lunches That Keep You Going 40

Mediterranean Chickpea Wraps 41

Quinoa and Roasted Veggie Bowl 42

Creamy Sweet Potato and Lentil Soup 43

Turkey and Avocado Grain Bowl 44

Hidden Veggie Turkey Meatballs 45

Spiced Lentil and Spinach Wraps 46

Rainbow Veggie Noodle Salad 47

Stuffed Bell Peppers with Quinoa and Black Beans 48

Avocado Tuna Salad Lettuce Wraps 49

Spicy Peanut Chicken and Veggie Stir-Fry 50

Sweet Potato and Kale Power Bowl 51

Curried Cauliflower Rice with Chickpeas 52

CHAPTER 4 53

Stealthy Dinners to Savor 53

Cheesy Cauliflower Crust Pizza 54

Zucchini Noodle Bolognese 55

Sweet Potato Shepherd's Pie 56

Black Bean and Quinoa Enchilada Casserole 57

Creamy Broccoli and White Bean Soup 58

Spaghetti Squash Pad Thai 59

Stuffed Bell Peppers with Lentils and Quinoa 60

Chickpea and Spinach Coconut Curry 61

Turkey and Veggie Meatloaf 62

Baked Salmon with Veggie-Loaded Pesto 63

CHAPTER 5 64

Snacks and Treats Made Healthy 64

Black Bean Brownies 65

Spinach Banana Smoothie 66

- Zucchini Muffins 67
- Avocado Chocolate Mousse 68
- Carrot Cake Energy Balls 69
- Sweet Potato Chocolate Chip Cookies 70
- Hidden Veggie Pita Chips with Hummus 71
- Beet and Berry Smoothie Popsicles 72
- Chickpea Blondies 73
- Apple Nachos with Nut Butter Drizzle 74

PART 3: ADVANCED MEAL PREP STRATEGIES 75

CHAPTER 6 76
- Customizing Meal Prep for Specific Needs 77
  - Plant-Based and Vegan-Friendly Options 77
  - Keto, Paleo, and Low-Carb Strategies 78
  - Gluten-Free and Allergy-Safe Meal Prep 78

CHAPTER 7 80
- Boosting Nutrient Absorption Through Smart Pairings 80

CHAPTER 8 83
- Streamlining Prep for Busy Lifestyles 83

PART 4: SUSTAINING YOUR STEALTH HEALTH JOURNEY 87

CHAPTER 9 88
- Creating a Sustainable Meal Prep Routine 88

CHAPTER 10 92
- Overcoming Common Challenges 92

CHAPTER 11 95
- Celebrating Progress 95

Conclusion 98

Appendices 100
- Pantry Staples for Stealth Health Success 100
- Meal Prep Shopping Lists by Recipe 100

  Quick Nutritional Reference Guide 102
BONUS SECTION 103
  BONUS 1 GLOSSARY TEMPLATE..103
BONUS 2 105
  Exclusive Meal Prep Tracker 105
BONUS 3 109
  DIY Spice Blends and Flavor Boosters 109
BONUS 4 111
  30-Minute Meal Prep Challenge 111
BONUS 5 114
  Conversion Charts.. 114

Stealth Health Cookbook

PREFACE

Meal prep has always fascinated me—not just as a concept, but as a lifeline during some of my busiest days. I vividly remember one chaotic week during my residency. My days started at 6 a.m. and ended when the stars were out. Eating healthy felt like an impossible dream, and takeout seemed to be my only option. One night, after yet another soggy sandwich and lukewarm coffee, I made a promise to myself: I would find a way to fuel my body with real, nourishing meals no matter how busy life became.

That small, determined step transformed my relationship with food. What began as a desperate experiment in batch-cooking has evolved into an art form, a science, and a tool that I'm passionate about sharing. This book is a reflection of that journey, shaped not just by my own experiences but by the stories of people I've encountered along the way—parents juggling work and kids, students on tight schedules, professionals chasing deadlines, and individuals striving to balance health with life's demands.

Why This Book Matters Now

In today's fast-paced world, eating well often takes a back seat. The pandemic shifted how we think about food, prompting many of us to cook at home more frequently, but sustaining those habits remains a challenge. According to recent research, nearly 60% of adults report feeling too busy to prepare healthy meals regularly. At the same time, interest in eating fresh, nutritious foods is at an all-time high. The disconnect is clear: we want better, healthier meals, but our schedules often stand in the way.

This book aims to bridge that gap by equipping you with tools, techniques, and recipes that fit into your life seamlessly. From crafting quick spice blends to embracing the 30-minute meal prep challenge, you'll discover that healthy eating doesn't have to mean sacrificing time or flavor.

Personal Touch, Universal Value

What makes this journey special is its universality. We've all faced those moments: staring into the fridge, too tired to think, let alone cook. But with a bit of planning and creativity, that tired moment can become an opportunity. This book isn't just about recipes; it's about empowerment. Each chapter offers actionable advice tailored to real-life challenges, with tips for everyone—from the kitchen novice to the seasoned home chef.

The joy of meal prep isn't just in saving time or cutting costs. It's in the way it simplifies life, creates space for creativity, and allows you to focus on what truly matters. Imagine walking into your kitchen and knowing exactly what's for dinner—or better yet, having it ready to heat and serve.

An Invitation

This book is more than a guide; it's a conversation. I encourage you to experiment, adapt, and make these methods your own. Share your successes, your challenges, and your favorite meals with your loved ones—and maybe even on social media! You'll be surprised how quickly these small changes can ripple into something transformative.

Whether you're here to cut grocery costs, improve your health, or rediscover the joy of eating, this book will be your companion. Together, we'll turn meal prep from a chore into a lifestyle—one flavorful, nourishing dish at a time.

Let's get started, and let the journey to a healthier, tastier life begin.

INTRODUCTION

Imagine sitting at the dinner table with your family, enjoying a hearty lasagna. The sauce is rich, the cheese perfectly melted, and the flavors balanced to perfection. Unbeknownst to anyone, the sauce is brimming with pureed carrots and spinach, the pasta is whole-grain, and the cheesy topping includes protein-packed Greek yogurt. Everyone leaves the table satisfied, none the wiser that they just consumed a meal packed with hidden nutrition. This, in essence, is *Stealth Health*: the art of subtly enhancing meals to boost their nutritional value without compromising flavor or enjoyment.

Stealth Health isn't about drastic diet overhauls or forcing kale smoothies on unsuspecting eaters. Instead, it's a lifestyle shift that embraces small, sustainable changes. It's about recognizing that nutrition doesn't have to scream its presence; it can quietly enhance every meal, improving health outcomes while still delighting the palate. Let's uncover how this approach can transform your cooking and set the foundation for long-term wellness.

What is Stealth Health?

Stealth Health is a culinary strategy rooted in subtlety and creativity. At its core, it involves integrating nutrient-dense ingredients into everyday meals in a way that goes unnoticed by the eater. While the term may sound like a marketing gimmick, the concept has deep scientific and psychological underpinnings.

The genius of Stealth Health lies in its simplicity. By adding grated zucchini to a pasta sauce, blending cauliflower into mashed potatoes, or using avocado to make creamy desserts, you're enriching dishes with vitamins, minerals, and fiber. The best part? Picky eaters, children, or even skeptical adults won't detect these enhancements because they're seamlessly integrated into the dish's natural texture and flavor profile.

This approach not only works but also empowers individuals to make healthier choices without feeling restricted or deprived. Unlike traditional "diet food" that often sacrifices taste for nutrition, Stealth Health is about balance—delivering deliciousness with a side of good health.

Sneaking Nutrition into Everyday Meals

Cooking with Stealth Health is like playing a fun culinary game. The goal? Boost nutrition in every bite. Here's how:

1. **Pureed Vegetables**: Spinach, carrots, and squash can be pureed and added to sauces, soups, and casseroles. Their mild flavors blend effortlessly, making them virtually undetectable.

2. **Alternative Flours**: Swap regular flour with almond, oat, or chickpea flour in baked goods to increase protein and fiber without altering taste significantly.

3. **Healthy Fats**: Use mashed avocado or Greek yogurt as substitutes for butter or cream in recipes. These swaps add heart-healthy fats and cut down on saturated fats.

4. **Superfood Additions**: Incorporate chia seeds, flaxseeds, or nutritional yeast into batters, smoothies, or even popcorn for added nutrients.

5. **Sweet Alternatives**: Replace refined sugar with natural sweeteners like honey, maple syrup, or mashed bananas. This reduces sugar spikes while maintaining sweetness.

By using these techniques, you're not just cooking—you're crafting meals that fuel the body and taste amazing. The stealthy approach is particularly helpful for families where health-conscious parents might struggle to get their kids (or partners) to eat more vegetables.

The Benefits of Hidden Nutrition for You and Your Family

Stealth Health is more than a strategy—it's a tool for building healthier habits. Here's how it benefits everyone at the table:

- **Improved Nutritional Intake**: Hidden vegetables and nutrient-rich substitutes increase fiber, vitamins, and minerals in the diet without additional effort.

- **Supports Healthy Weight Management**: By replacing calorie-dense ingredients with lighter, nutrient-dense options, meals are more filling and balanced.

- **Reduces Resistance to Healthy Eating**: Many people resist "healthy food" due to preconceived notions about taste. Stealth Health eliminates this barrier by making nutritious meals enjoyable.

- **Builds Long-Term Habits**: Over time, the subtle inclusion of healthier ingredients conditions taste buds to appreciate a broader range of foods.

For families, Stealth Health fosters a positive relationship with food, demonstrating that nutritious eating doesn't have to feel like a chore. It encourages creativity in the kitchen and opens the door to experimenting with flavors and textures.

The Basics of Meal Prep

Why Meal Prep Matters

Life is busy, and when hunger strikes, convenience often wins. Unfortunately, convenience foods are rarely the healthiest choice. Enter meal prep: a practical solution that combines efficiency with mindful eating. When meals are planned and prepared in advance, it reduces the likelihood of reaching for processed snacks or takeout.

Meal prep allows you to:

- Control ingredients and portions.
- Save money by reducing food waste.
- Maintain consistency in healthy eating habits.
- Save time during busy weekdays.

With Stealth Health as your guiding principle, meal prep becomes even more impactful. By planning stealthy recipes ahead of time, you're setting yourself up for nutritional success all week long.

Tools and Essentials for Efficient Meal Prep

To master Stealth Health meal prep, you need the right tools. These essentials make the process smoother and more enjoyable:

1. **Quality Containers**: Invest in leak-proof, stackable containers. Glass options are ideal for reheating and preserving flavors.
2. **Sharp Knives**: A good set of knives speeds up chopping and ensures precision.
3. **Blender or Food Processor**: Perfect for pureeing vegetables or making healthy sauces and dips.
4. **Sheet Pans and Baking Dishes**: Essential for batch cooking and roasting.
5. **Spice Rack**: Stock your pantry with spices and herbs to enhance flavors without relying on salt or sugar.

6. **Measuring Tools**: Accurate measurements are key to maintaining balance in recipes.

7. **Slow Cooker or Instant Pot**: These appliances are game-changers for hands-off cooking and creating large batches.

By organizing your kitchen and equipping it with these essentials, you'll find meal prep more efficient and enjoyable.

Why Stealth Health and Meal Prep Work Together

Stealth Health and meal prep are a match made in culinary heaven. When you combine the creativity of sneaking nutrition into dishes with the practicality of prepping meals in advance, you're creating a sustainable routine that benefits your health and lifestyle. This synergy not only saves time but also ensures that your meals are nutritious, delicious, and ready when you need them most.

As you embark on this journey, remember that Stealth Health isn't about perfection. It's about progress—small, thoughtful changes that lead to big, lasting results. Whether you're preparing meals for a busy week or trying to please a family of picky eaters, the principles of Stealth Health will empower you to make every bite count.

PART 1: FOUNDATIONS OF STEALTH HEALTH MEAL PREP

CHAPTER 1

The Essentials of Meal Prep

Preparing meals in advance can seem daunting at first, but the right tools, setup, and mindset can transform your kitchen into a productivity hub. This section will help you get started by covering the key essentials for efficient and stress-free meal prep.

Setting Up Your Kitchen for Success

A well-organized kitchen is the foundation of successful meal prep. Imagine walking into a space where everything you need is easily accessible, and clutter doesn't slow you down. Here's how to get there:

1. Declutter and Streamline

Start by clearing your countertops of unnecessary appliances and tools. Keep only the essentials within arm's reach. For instance:

2. Store rarely used gadgets in cabinets or drawers.

Create dedicated zones for chopping, cooking, and storage to reduce back-and-forth movement.

3. Keep Ingredients Organized

Group pantry items by category: grains, canned goods, spices, and snacks. Use clear containers to store items like flour, rice, or nuts so you can see what's inside at a glance. Labeling containers ensures you know what you have and prevents overbuying.

4. Maximize Refrigerator Space

Invest in stackable containers or bins to organize your fridge. Dedicate specific shelves for prepped meals, raw ingredients, and leftovers. Use the "first in, first out" system to minimize waste.

5. Plan a Workspace Layout

Make sure your workspace has ample room for chopping, mixing, and assembling meals. Keep a cutting board, knife block, and frequently used utensils in this area. A clean, open workspace is key to speeding up your prep sessions.

Must-Have Tools and Containers

Equipping your kitchen with the right tools will save you time and effort. Here are the essentials every meal prepper should have:

1. **High-Quality Knives**

A sharp chef's knife and a paring knife are non-negotiable. They speed up chopping and slicing, ensuring consistent results. A knife sharpener or honing steel is also vital to keep your tools in top shape.

2. **Cutting Boards**

Use separate cutting boards for raw proteins and vegetables to prevent cross-contamination. Opt for large, durable boards with non-slip grips to make chopping easier.

3. **Measuring Tools**

Accurate measuring spoons, cups, and a kitchen scale are crucial for portioning ingredients and following recipes.

4. **Mixing Bowls**

A set of nesting mixing bowls in various sizes is perfect for mixing, tossing, and holding ingredients.

Cookware

Essentials include:

- Non-stick and stainless-steel pans for cooking proteins and veggies.
- A stockpot for soups, stews, or grains.
- A slow cooker or Instant Pot for hands-off batch cooking.

Storage Containers

Invest in BPA-free, airtight containers in various sizes. Glass containers are durable and microwave-safe, while stackable plastic ones save space. Divide containers into single-serving sizes to make grab-and-go meals easier.

Baking Sheets and Silicone Mats

- Baking sheets are versatile for roasting veggies or cooking proteins. Silicone mats make cleanup a breeze and reduce waste from parchment paper.

Food Processor or Blender

- These are invaluable for quickly chopping vegetables, making sauces, or preparing smoothies.

Batch Cooking Basics

Batch cooking is the cornerstone of meal prep. It involves preparing large quantities of food at once, which can be portioned and stored for later use. Here's how to master it:

Choose Versatile Recipes

Focus on dishes that can be used in multiple ways. For example:

- Roasted vegetables can top salads, be blended into soups, or serve as sides.
- Grilled chicken works in wraps, pasta, or rice bowls.

Cook in Bulk

- Dedicate one day a week to cooking several recipes at once. This could include making a pot of soup, roasting proteins, and prepping grains like quinoa or brown rice.

Portion Strategically

- Divide cooked food into individual servings to avoid overeating or wasting leftovers. Label each container with the date it was prepared to ensure freshness.

Store Smartly

- Use freezer-friendly containers for items like soups, stews, or casseroles. Vacuum-sealing bags are great for preserving proteins or produce for extended periods.

Rotate Ingredients

- Keep meals interesting by rotating proteins, grains, and vegetables each week. This prevents monotony while ensuring balanced nutrition.

Mastering these essentials will make meal prep an enjoyable and rewarding habit. Not only will you save time and reduce stress, but you'll also create a kitchen environment that supports your health goals. Once your kitchen is equipped and organized, the possibilities are endless!

Healthy Swaps Made Easy

Making healthier food choices doesn't mean sacrificing taste or satisfaction. It's about being strategic with your ingredients, finding clever ways to boost nutrition, and maintaining the flavors you love. Here, we'll explore practical swaps, creative ways to sneak in nutrients, and simple hacks to cut down on sugar, salt, and fat without compromising on enjoyment.

Replacing Refined Ingredients Without Sacrificing Taste

Refined ingredients like white flour, sugar, and processed fats are staples in many recipes, but they often lack nutrients. Swapping these out for healthier alternatives is easier than you think.

1. **Flour Alternatives**
    - **Whole Wheat Flour:** Use in place of white flour in baked goods for added fiber and nutrients. Start with a 50/50 mix to ease into the change.
    - **Almond or Coconut Flour:** Perfect for gluten-free or low-carb diets. These add a nutty flavor and work well in pancakes or muffins.
    - **Oat Flour:** Easily made by blending oats, this adds a hearty texture and boosts soluble fiber, which supports heart health.

2. **Healthier Sweeteners**
    - **Honey or Maple Syrup:** Natural sweeteners that offer trace nutrients. Use less than the recipe calls for, as they're sweeter than sugar.
    - **Mashed Bananas or Applesauce:** These add natural sweetness to baked goods while reducing the need for added sugar and fats.
    - **Stevia or Monk Fruit Extract:** Calorie-free and plant-based, these sweeteners are ideal for cutting sugar without losing sweetness.

3. **Healthier Fats**
    - **Avocado:** Use mashed avocado instead of butter in spreads or baked goods for a creamy texture and heart-healthy fats.
    - **Greek Yogurt:** A fantastic substitute for sour cream, mayo, or heavy cream. It cuts calories while adding protein and creaminess.
    - **Coconut Oil:** A flavorful alternative to butter in recipes like cookies or pancakes. Use sparingly, as it's calorie-dense.

The Art of Adding Hidden Vegetables and Nutrients

Vegetables are often underutilized in recipes, but with a few tricks, you can pack meals with vitamins and fiber without anyone noticing.

1. **Pureed Vegetables**

    - **Cauliflower:** Blend steamed cauliflower into mashed potatoes, mac and cheese, or creamy soups for extra fiber and vitamin C.

    - **Zucchini:** Grated zucchini adds moisture to baked goods like muffins or brownies while boosting their nutritional profile.

    - **Carrots and Sweet Potatoes:** These can be pureed and added to tomato sauces, pancake batter, or even grilled cheese sandwiches for subtle sweetness and extra beta-carotene.

2. **Leafy Greens**

    - Blend spinach or kale into smoothies, soups, or pasta sauces. Their flavor becomes almost undetectable when combined with strong ingredients like fruits or tomatoes.

3. **Legumes and Beans**

    - Use black beans or chickpeas in brownies or cookie dough for added protein and fiber. They create a fudgy texture and keep the sweetness intact.

    - Add lentils to meat-based dishes like tacos or Bolognese sauce to reduce the meat portion and add plant-based nutrients.

Simple Hacks to Cut Sugar, Salt, and Fat

1. **Cutting Sugar Without Losing Sweetness**

- **Cinnamon and Vanilla:** Enhance natural sweetness in oatmeal, coffee, or baked goods without adding sugar.
- **Roasting Fruits:** Caramelize the natural sugars in fruits like apples, pears, or peaches by roasting them. Use these as toppings for yogurt or pancakes.
- **Dilute Juices:** If you enjoy fruit juice, mix it with sparkling water to reduce sugar while keeping it refreshing.

2. **Reducing Salt Without Sacrificing Flavor**

- **Herbs and Spices:** Use garlic, onion powder, smoked paprika, or fresh herbs like parsley and cilantro to add layers of flavor.
- **Citrus Zest and Juice:** Lemon or lime zest can brighten dishes and reduce the need for added salt.
- **Low-Sodium Alternatives:** Opt for reduced-sodium versions of soy sauce, broth, and canned goods.

3. **Trimming Unhealthy Fats**

- **Air Frying or Baking:** Replace deep frying with air frying or baking for crispy results without excess oil.
- **Broth Instead of Oil:** Sauté vegetables in broth or water instead of oil to cut calories.
- **Egg Whites:** Use egg whites instead of whole eggs in recipes to reduce cholesterol and fat.

Making these swaps and hacks a part of your routine will create meals that nourish your body without sacrificing enjoyment. These small changes add up to significant improvements in health while keeping your food flavorful and satisfying.

Mastering Flavor the Healthy Way

Healthy eating doesn't have to mean bland, boring meals. The secret lies in learning how to use herbs, spices, and natural flavor enhancers to create dishes that excite the palate while nourishing the body. By tapping into a rich world of seasonings and culinary techniques, you can build layers of flavor that elevate your cooking without relying on excess salt, sugar, or fat. Here's how to make healthy food taste irresistible.

Using Herbs, Spices, and Natural Flavor Enhancers

1. **Herbs: The Fresh and Fragrant Boost**
   Herbs are the easiest way to add freshness and complexity to your dishes. Use fresh or dried versions depending on the dish, but remember that fresh herbs add brightness while dried herbs offer concentrated flavors.

   - **Basil and Oregano:** Perfect for Italian dishes, pair these with tomatoes, garlic, and olive oil for a classic Mediterranean taste.
   - **Cilantro:** Adds a citrusy note to Mexican, Thai, or Indian cuisine. Chop it fresh for salsas, curries, and soups.
   - **Rosemary and Thyme:** These woody herbs are excellent for roasting vegetables, poultry, or potatoes. Crush slightly to release their oils.

2. **Spices: The Bold and Aromatic Heroes**
   Spices transform simple ingredients into vibrant meals. Toasting whole spices or "blooming" them in oil amplifies their potency.

   - **Cumin and Coriander:** Ground or whole, these spices add warmth to soups, stews, and roasted vegetables.
   - **Turmeric:** Known for its earthy, slightly bitter flavor and golden hue, turmeric pairs well with ginger in curries, rice dishes, and teas.
   - **Paprika and Smoked Paprika:** Add depth to grilled meats, roasted chickpeas, or deviled eggs.

3. **Natural Flavor Enhancers**
   Instead of relying on salt, sugar, or butter for flavor, try these healthier alternatives:

- **Citrus:** Lemon juice, lime zest, and orange segments brighten up salads, marinades, and dressings.
- **Vinegars:** Balsamic, apple cider, and rice vinegar add tanginess to dishes without extra calories. Use them in dressings, stir-fries, or glazes.
- **Nutritional Yeast:** A savory, cheese-like powder perfect for sprinkling on popcorn, pasta, or roasted veggies.

Techniques for Making Healthy Food Taste Irresistible

1. **Layering Flavors**

   Build flavor at every stage of cooking. Start with aromatic bases like onions, garlic, or shallots, then add spices and finish with fresh herbs or a squeeze of citrus. For instance:

   - Sauté onions and garlic in olive oil for depth.
   - Add cumin and smoked paprika for warmth.
   - Finish with cilantro and lime juice for brightness.

2. **Marination and Infusion**

   Marinate proteins like chicken, tofu, or fish in mixtures of yogurt, citrus juice, and spices to tenderize and flavor them. For an infusion, steep herbs like rosemary in olive oil for a custom dressing or drizzle.

3. **Roasting for Richness**

   Roasting vegetables and proteins caramelizes their natural sugars, intensifying flavor. Toss vegetables like carrots, brussels sprouts, or cauliflower in olive oil and seasonings before roasting for a sweet-savory punch.

4. **Balancing the Five Tastes**

   Every great dish balances sweet, salty, sour, bitter, and umami.

   - **Sweet:** Add honey, balsamic glaze, or roasted fruits.
   - **Salty:** Use sea salt sparingly or replace it with miso paste or low-sodium soy sauce.
   - **Sour:** Brighten dishes with vinegar or citrus.
   - **Bitter:** Include arugula, kale, or dark chocolate for balance.
   - **Umami:** Use mushrooms, tomatoes, or nutritional yeast to enhance depth.

5. **Garnishing with Purpose**
   The final touch can make or break a dish. Add freshly chopped herbs, toasted seeds, or a drizzle of flavored oil to take your meals from good to gourmet.

By mastering the use of herbs, spices, and natural enhancers, you can transform your meals into culinary delights that are as healthy as they are satisfying. These techniques not only make your food taste better but also turn cooking into an enjoyable, creative process.

PART 2: STEALTHY RECIPES FOR EVERY MEAL

CHAPTER 2
Energizing Breakfasts with a Twist

Spinach and Banana Pancakes

Serves: 4 (8 pancakes)

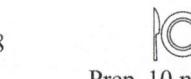
Prep. 10 mins

Easy

Cooking: 10 mins

COOKING STEPS

1. Blend spinach, banana, egg, oats, almond milk, vanilla, baking powder, and cinnamon in a blender until smooth.
2. Heat a non-stick skillet over medium heat and grease lightly with coconut oil.
3. Pour 1/4 cup batter for each pancake onto the skillet. Cook until bubbles form on the surface, about 2 minutes, then flip and cook for 1 more minute.
4. Serve warm with fresh fruit or a drizzle of honey.

INGREDIENTS

1 cup fresh spinach (packed)
1 ripe banana
1 large egg
1 cup rolled oats
1/2 cup unsweetened almond milk
1 tsp vanilla extract
1 tsp baking powder
1/2 tsp cinnamon
Coconut oil for cooking

Nutritional information:
Calories: 90 | Protein: 4g | Carbs: 13g | Fat: 3g | Fiber: 2g

Carrot Cake Muffins

 Serves: 12 muffins

 Prep. 15 mins

 Easy

 Cooking: 20 mins

COOKING STEPS

1. Preheat oven to 350°F (175°C). Line a muffin tin with paper liners.
2. In a large bowl, whisk flour, baking powder, baking soda, salt, cinnamon, nutmeg, and flaxseed.
3. In a separate bowl, mix carrots, maple syrup, applesauce, coconut oil, eggs, and vanilla. Gradually add dry ingredients, stirring until just combined.
4. Divide batter evenly among muffin cups. Bake for 20 minutes or until a toothpick inserted in the center comes out clean.
5. Cool for 5 minutes in the pan, then transfer to a wire rack.

INGREDIENTS

1 1/2 cups whole wheat flour
1 tsp baking powder
1/2 tsp baking soda
1/2 tsp salt
1 tsp cinnamon
1/4 tsp nutmeg
1/4 cup ground flaxseed
2 cups grated carrots
1/3 cup maple syrup
1/2 cup unsweetened applesauce
1/4 cup melted coconut oil
2 large eggs
1 tsp vanilla extract

Nutritional information:
Calories: 120 | Protein: 3g | Carbs: 18g | Fat: 5g | Fiber: 3g

Avocado and Berry Smoothie Bowl

 Serves: 02

 Prep. 5 mins

 Easy

 Cooking: 0 mins

COOKING STEPS

1. Blend avocado, berries, banana, almond milk, chia seeds, and honey (if using) until thick and creamy.
2. Pour into a bowl and top with granola, almonds, and coconut.

INGREDIENTS

1/2 avocado
1 cup frozen mixed berries
1/2 frozen banana
1 cup unsweetened almond milk
1 tbsp chia seeds
1 tbsp honey (optional)
Toppings: granola, sliced almonds, shredded coconut

Nutritional information:
Calories: 210 | Protein: 4g | Carbs: 28g | Fat: 9g | Fiber: 7g

Sweet Potato Breakfast Hash

 Serves: 04

 Prep. 10 mins

 Easy

 Cooking: 15 mins

COOKING STEPS

1. Heat olive oil in a large skillet over medium heat. Add sweet potatoes and cook for 8–10 minutes, stirring occasionally.
2. Add onion and bell pepper. Cook until softened, about 5 minutes.
3. Toss in kale and smoked paprika, cooking until wilted. Season with salt and pepper.

INGREDIENTS

2 medium sweet potatoes, diced
1 small onion, chopped
1 bell pepper, diced
2 cups kale, chopped
2 tbsp olive oil
1 tsp smoked paprika
Salt and pepper to taste

Nutritional information:
Calories: 180 | Protein: 3g | Carbs: 28g | Fat: 7g | Fiber: 5g

Zucchini and Chocolate Chip Muffins

Serves: 12 muffins

Prep. 15 mins

Easy

Cooking: 20 mins

COOKING STEPS

1. Preheat the oven to 350°F (175°C). Line a muffin tin with paper liners.
2. In a bowl, mix almond flour, oat flour, baking soda, cinnamon, and salt.
3. In another bowl, whisk eggs, maple syrup, coconut oil, and vanilla. Fold in zucchini and dry ingredients. Stir in chocolate chips.
4. Divide batter evenly into the muffin tin. Bake for 18–20 minutes or until a toothpick comes out clean.

INGREDIENTS

1 1/2 cups almond flour
1/2 cup oat flour
1 tsp baking soda
1/2 tsp cinnamon
1/4 tsp salt
1/2 cup grated zucchini (squeezed to remove excess moisture)
1/3 cup dark chocolate chips
1/3 cup maple syrup
2 large eggs
1/4 cup melted coconut oil
1 tsp vanilla extract

Nutritional information:

Calories: 140 | Protein: 4g | Carbs: 12g | Fat: 9g | Fiber: 2g

Cauliflower Breakfast Scramble

 Serves: 02

 Prep. 10 mins

 Easy

 Cooking: 10 mins

COOKING STEPS

1. Heat olive oil in a skillet over medium heat. Add onions and bell peppers, sauté until softened.
2. Stir in cauliflower rice and turmeric. Cook for 3–4 minutes.
3. Push mixture to one side of the skillet, scramble the eggs on the other side, then combine. Season with salt and pepper.

INGREDIENTS

1 cup cauliflower rice
2 large eggs
1/4 cup diced onions
1/4 cup diced bell peppers
1 tbsp olive oil
1/2 tsp turmeric
Salt and pepper to taste

Nutritional information:

Calories: 180 | Protein: 10g | Carbs: 6g | Fat: 12g | Fiber: 2g

Pumpkin Spice Overnight Oats

Serves: 02

Prep. 5 mins

Easy

Cooking: Overnight

COOKING STEPS

1. Combine oats, pumpkin puree, almond milk, chia seeds, pumpkin spice, and maple syrup in a jar or bowl. Mix well.
2. Refrigerate overnight. In the morning, top with pecans and cranberries before serving.

INGREDIENTS

1 cup rolled oats
1/2 cup pumpkin puree
1 1/4 cups almond milk
1 tbsp chia seeds
1 tsp pumpkin spice
1 tbsp maple syrup
Toppings: pecans, dried cranberries

Nutritional information:

Calories: 240 | Protein: 6g | Carbs: 38g | Fat: 7g | Fiber: 8g

Quinoa Breakfast Bowl with Pomegranate and Nuts

Serves: 02

Prep. 10 mins

Easy

Cooking: 15 mins

Cooking Steps

1. Warm quinoa and almond milk in a saucepan over medium heat. Stir in honey and cinnamon.
2. Serve in bowls, topped with pomegranate seeds and almonds.

Ingredients

1 cup cooked quinoa
1/2 cup unsweetened almond milk
1 tbsp honey
1/2 tsp cinnamon
1/4 cup pomegranate seeds
2 tbsp chopped almonds

Nutritional information:

Calories: 220 | Protein: 7g | Carbs: 32g | Fat: 7g | Fiber: 4g

Sweet Beet and Berry Smoothie

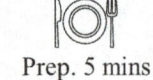

Serves: 01 | Prep. 5 mins | Easy | Cooking: 0 mins

COOKING STEPS

1. Blend beet, berries, banana, coconut water, and flaxseed until smooth. Pour into glasses and serve chilled.

INGREDIENTS

1 small cooked beet
1 cup frozen mixed berries
1/2 frozen banana
1 cup unsweetened coconut water
1 tbsp ground flaxseed

Nutritional information:

Calories: 120 | Protein: 3g | Carbs: 26g | Fat: 1g | Fiber: 5g

Hidden Veggie Breakfast Wraps

Serves: 02 | Prep. 10 mins | Easy | Cooking: 10 mins

Cooking Steps

2. Heat olive oil in a skillet and sauté zucchini and carrots until softened.
3. Add scrambled eggs and cook until set.
4. Divide the mixture between tortillas, sprinkle with cheese, and roll into wraps.

Ingredients

2 whole-grain tortillas
1/2 cup grated zucchini
1/4 cup shredded carrots
2 large eggs, scrambled
2 tbsp shredded cheese
1 tbsp olive oil
Salt and pepper to taste

Nutritional information:

Calories: 200 | Protein: 9g | Carbs: 22g | Fat: 8g | Fiber: 4g

Stealth Health Cookbook

CHAPTER 3
Lunches That Keep You Going

Mediterranean Chickpea Wraps

Serves: 4 wraps

Prep. 15 mins

Easy

Cooking: none

COOKING STEPS

1. In a bowl, toss chickpeas, cucumber, tomatoes, olive oil, and lemon juice. Season with salt and pepper.
2. Spread hummus on each tortilla. Add the chickpea mixture and sprinkle with feta. Roll tightly into wraps.
3. Wrap individually in foil for easy meal prep.

INGREDIENTS

4 whole-grain tortillas
1 cup canned chickpeas (rinsed and drained)
1/2 cup diced cucumber
1/2 cup halved cherry tomatoes
1/4 cup crumbled feta cheese
2 tbsp hummus
1 tbsp olive oil
1 tsp lemon juice
Salt and pepper to taste

Nutritional information:
Calories: 250 | Protein: 8g | Carbs: 32g | Fat: 9g | Fiber: 6g

Quinoa and Roasted Veggie Bowl

Serves: 04 | Prep. 10 mins | Easy | Cooking: 25 mins

Cooking Steps

1. Preheat oven to 400°F (200°C). Toss vegetables with olive oil and smoked paprika. Roast for 20–25 minutes.
2. Divide quinoa into four containers. Top with roasted veggies.
3. In a small bowl, whisk tahini, lemon juice, and 2 tbsp water. Drizzle over bowls before serving.

Ingredients

1 cup quinoa, cooked
2 cups mixed roasted vegetables (zucchini, bell peppers, and sweet potatoes)
1/4 cup tahini
2 tbsp lemon juice
1 tbsp olive oil
1 tsp smoked paprika
Salt and pepper to taste

Nutritional information:
Calories: 280 | Protein: 7g | Carbs: 35g | Fat: 12g | Fiber: 5g

Creamy Sweet Potato and Lentil Soup

Serves: 04
Prep. 15 mins
Easy
Cooking: 30 mins

COOKING STEPS

1. In a large pot, sauté onions and garlic until fragrant. Add cumin and turmeric.
2. Stir in lentils, sweet potato, and broth. Bring to a boil, then simmer for 25 minutes.
3. Blend half the soup for a creamy texture while leaving some chunks for texture.

INGREDIENTS

1 cup red lentils
1 medium sweet potato, diced
1 small onion, chopped
2 garlic cloves, minced
4 cups vegetable broth
1 tsp cumin
1/2 tsp turmeric
Salt and pepper to taste

Nutritional information:
Calories: 210 | Protein: 12g | Carbs: 38g | Fat: 2g | Fiber: 10g

Turkey and Avocado Grain Bowl

Serves: 04 | Prep. 10 mins | Easy | Cooking: None

Cooking Steps

1. Divide rice or farro into bowls. Layer with turkey, avocado, carrots, and sesame seeds.
2. Drizzle with soy sauce and rice vinegar.

Ingredients

2 cups cooked brown rice or farro
1 cup shredded turkey breast
1 avocado, sliced
1/2 cup shredded carrots
2 tbsp sesame seeds
3 tbsp low-sodium soy sauce
1 tbsp rice vinegar

Nutritional information:
Calories: 340 | Protein: 20g | Carbs: 38g | Fat: 12g | Fiber: 6g

Hidden Veggie Turkey Meatballs

Serves: 04 | Prep. 20 mins | Easy | Cooking: 25 mins

COOKING STEPS

1. Preheat oven to 375°F (190°C).
2. Combine all ingredients in a bowl. Form into meatballs.
3. Bake on a lined tray for 20–25 minutes. Pair with whole-grain pasta or salad.

INGREDIENTS

1 lb ground turkey
1/2 cup grated zucchini (squeezed dry)
1/2 cup grated carrots
1/4 cup breadcrumbs
1 egg
1 tsp garlic powder
Salt and pepper to taste

Nutritional information:
Calories: 220 | Protein: 25g | Carbs: 8g | Fat: 10g | Fiber: 2g

Spiced Lentil and Spinach Wraps

Serves: 04 | Prep. 15 mins | Easy | Cooking: 10 mins

Cooking Steps

1. Heat lentils in a skillet with curry powder and garlic powder. Stir in spinach until wilted.
2. Spread yogurt on tortillas. Add lentil mixture and roll tightly.

Ingredients

1 cup cooked lentils
1 cup spinach, chopped
4 whole-grain tortillas
1/2 cup Greek yogurt
1 tsp curry powder
1/2 tsp garlic powder

Nutritional information:
Calories: 240 | Protein: 10g | Carbs: 36g | Fat: 5g | Fiber: 7g

Rainbow Veggie Noodle Salad

Serves: 04
Prep. 15 mins
Easy
Cooking: none

COOKING STEPS

1. Combine all vegetables in a large bowl.
2. In a small bowl, whisk together rice vinegar, soy sauce, and sesame oil.
3. Toss the vegetables with the dressing and sprinkle with sesame seeds before serving.

INGREDIENTS

1 zucchini, spiralized
1 carrot, spiralized
1/2 red bell pepper, thinly sliced
1/2 yellow bell pepper, thinly sliced
1 cup shredded purple cabbage
2 tbsp sesame seeds
3 tbsp rice vinegar
2 tbsp soy sauce
1 tsp sesame oil

Nutritional information:
Calories: 100 | Protein: 3g | Carbs: 15g | Fat: 4g | Fiber: 5g

Stuffed Bell Peppers with Quinoa and Black Beans

Serves: 04 | Prep. 20 mins | Easy | Cooking: 30 mins

Cooking Steps

1. Preheat oven to 375°F (190°C).
2. In a bowl, combine quinoa, black beans, tomatoes, cumin, and chili powder.
3. Stuff the peppers with the mixture and place in a baking dish.
4. Sprinkle cheese on top (if using) and bake for 30 minutes.

Ingredients

4 large bell peppers, tops removed and seeds scooped out
1 cup cooked quinoa
1 cup black beans, rinsed and drained
1/2 cup diced tomatoes
1/2 cup shredded cheddar cheese (optional)
1 tsp cumin
1/2 tsp chili powder
Salt and pepper to taste

Nutritional information:
Calories: 220 | Protein: 9g | Carbs: 35g | Fat: 5g | Fiber: 7g

Avocado Tuna Salad Lettuce Wraps

Serves: 04 | Prep. 10 mins | Easy | Cooking: None

COOKING STEPS

1. In a bowl, mix tuna, mashed avocado, onion, celery, and lemon juice until well combined.
2. Scoop the mixture onto lettuce leaves and serve as wraps.

INGREDIENTS

2 cans tuna in water, drained
1 avocado, mashed
1/4 cup diced red onion
1/4 cup diced celery
1 tbsp lemon juice
8 large romaine lettuce leaves

Nutritional information:

Calories: 180 | Protein: 20g | Carbs: 4g | Fat: 8g | Fiber: 3g

Spicy Peanut Chicken and Veggie Stir-Fry

Serves: 04 | Prep. 10 mins | Easy | Cooking: 15 mins

COOKING STEPS

1. Heat a nonstick skillet over medium heat. Sauté chicken until cooked through.
2. Add vegetables and cook for 5–7 minutes until tender.
3. In a small bowl, whisk peanut butter, soy sauce, sriracha, and honey.
4. Pour the sauce over the stir-fry and toss until coated.

INGREDIENTS

1 lb chicken breast, diced
2 cups broccoli florets
1 cup snap peas
1 red bell pepper, sliced
1/4 cup natural peanut butter
2 tbsp soy sauce
1 tbsp sriracha
1 tsp honey

Nutritional information:
Calories: 300 | Protein: 28g | Carbs: 12g | Fat: 15g | Fiber: 4g

Sweet Potato and Kale Power Bowl

Serves: 04
Prep. 10 mins
Easy
Cooking: 25 mins

COOKING STEPS

1. Roast sweet potatoes at 400°F (200°C) for 25 minutes.
2. Toss kale in a hot skillet until slightly wilted.
3. Combine sweet potatoes, kale, and lentils in bowls.
4. Whisk tahini, maple syrup, and paprika, then drizzle over bowls.

INGREDIENTS

2 medium sweet potatoes, diced
2 cups kale, chopped
1/2 cup cooked lentils
1/4 cup tahini
1 tbsp maple syrup
1 tsp smoked paprika

Nutritional information:

Calories: 260 | Protein: 10g | Carbs: 38g | Fat: 8g | Fiber: 8g

Curried Cauliflower Rice with Chickpeas

Serves: 04
Prep. 15 mins
Easy
Cooking: 10 mins

Cooking Steps

1. In a skillet, heat cauliflower rice until softened.
2. Add chickpeas, tomatoes, coconut milk, curry powder, and turmeric.
3. Cook for 5–7 minutes until heated through.

Ingredients

2 cups cauliflower rice
1 cup chickpeas, rinsed and drained
1/2 cup diced tomatoes
1/4 cup coconut milk
1 tsp curry powder
1/2 tsp turmeric

Nutritional information:
Calories: 190 | Protein: 6g | Carbs: 23g | Fat: 7g | Fiber: 5g

CHAPTER 4
Stealthy Dinners to Savor

Cheesy Cauliflower Crust Pizza

Serves: 04 | Prep. 20 mins | Easy | Cooking: 25 mins

Cooking Steps

1. Preheat the oven to 425°F (220°C).
2. Microwave the cauliflower rice for 5 minutes, then squeeze out excess water using a clean towel.
3. Mix cauliflower, mozzarella, Parmesan, egg, garlic powder, and oregano until dough-like.
4. Spread onto a parchment-lined baking sheet and bake for 12 minutes.
5. Add pizza sauce, vegetables, and more cheese if desired. Bake for another 10 minutes.

Ingredients

1 medium cauliflower head, riced (about 4 cups)
1/2 cup shredded mozzarella cheese
1/4 cup grated Parmesan cheese
1 egg, beaten
1/2 tsp garlic powder
1/4 tsp dried oregano
1/4 cup pizza sauce
1/2 cup fresh vegetables (e.g., bell peppers, mushrooms, spinach)

Nutritional information:

Calories: 150 | Protein: 10g | Carbs: 8g | Fat: 8g | Fiber: 2g

Zucchini Noodle Bolognese

Serves: 04
Prep. 15 mins
Easy
Cooking: 20 mins

COOKING STEPS

1. Heat olive oil in a skillet and sauté onions and garlic until fragrant.
2. Add ground turkey, cooking until browned. Stir in crushed tomatoes, Italian seasoning, salt, and pepper. Simmer for 15 minutes.
3. Steam zucchini noodles lightly for 2–3 minutes or serve raw for extra crunch.
4. Top noodles with the Bolognese sauce and garnish with fresh basil.

INGREDIENTS

4 medium zucchinis, spiralized
1 lb lean ground turkey or beef
1 can (14 oz) crushed tomatoes
1/2 cup diced onions
2 cloves garlic, minced
1 tsp Italian seasoning
Salt and pepper to taste
2 tbsp olive oil

Nutritional information:
Calories: 280 | Protein: 25g | Carbs: 10g | Fat: 15g | Fiber: 3g

Sweet Potato Shepherd's Pie

Serves: 06
Prep. 20 mins
Easy
Cooking: 30 mins

COOKING STEPS

1. Boil sweet potatoes until soft (about 15 minutes). Mash with salt and pepper.
2. Sauté ground chicken until browned. Add mixed vegetables, broth, tomato paste, and thyme. Simmer for 10 minutes.
3. Transfer the mixture to a baking dish and spread mashed sweet potatoes over the top.
4. Bake at 375°F (190°C) for 15 minutes.

INGREDIENTS

2 large sweet potatoes, peeled and diced
1 lb ground chicken or turkey
1 cup mixed vegetables (peas, carrots, and green beans)
1/2 cup chicken broth
2 tbsp tomato paste
1 tsp thyme
Salt and pepper to taste

Nutritional information:
Calories: 250 | Protein: 22g | Carbs: 25g | Fat: 6g | Fiber: 4g

Black Bean and Quinoa Enchilada Casserole

Serves: 06
Prep. 15 mins
Easy
Cooking: 25 mins

Cooking Steps

1. Preheat oven to 375°F (190°C).
2. Mix quinoa, black beans, corn, cumin, paprika, and half the cheese in a large bowl.
3. Pour into a greased casserole dish, top with enchilada sauce and remaining cheese.
4. Bake for 25 minutes until bubbly.

Ingredients

2 cups cooked quinoa
1 can (15 oz) black beans, rinsed and drained
1 cup corn kernels
1 cup enchilada sauce
1 cup shredded cheese
1/2 tsp cumin
1/2 tsp paprika

Nutritional information:
Calories: 290 | Protein: 13g | Carbs: 38g | Fat: 9g | Fiber: 8g

Creamy Broccoli and White Bean Soup

Serves: 04 | Prep. 10 mins | Easy | Cooking: 25 mins

COOKING STEPS

1. Heat olive oil and sauté garlic until fragrant. Add broccoli and cook for 5 minutes.
2. Stir in cannellini beans, broth, and almond milk. Simmer for 15 minutes.
3. Use an immersion blender to blend until creamy. Serve warm.

INGREDIENTS

4 cups broccoli florets
1 can (15 oz) cannellini beans, rinsed and drained
2 cups vegetable broth
1 cup unsweetened almond milk
2 cloves garlic, minced
1 tbsp olive oil

Nutritional information:
Calories: 180 | Protein: 10g | Carbs: 20g | Fat: 7g | Fiber: 5g

Spaghetti Squash Pad Thai

Serves: 04
Prep. 15 mins
Easy
Cooking: 25 mins

Cooking Steps

1. Preheat oven to 400°F (200°C). Cut the spaghetti squash in half, scoop out the seeds, and bake cut side down for 25 minutes.
2. Use a fork to scrape out the spaghetti-like strands.
3. In a large skillet, heat sesame oil and scramble eggs. Add carrots, bean sprouts, and squash.
4. Mix soy sauce, lime juice, and peanut butter; pour over the squash mixture and toss. Garnish with green onions and crushed peanuts.

Ingredients

1 medium spaghetti squash
1 cup shredded carrots
1/2 cup bean sprouts
1/3 cup chopped green onions
1/4 cup crushed peanuts
2 eggs, lightly beaten
3 tbsp soy sauce or coconut aminos
2 tbsp lime juice
1 tbsp peanut butter
1 tsp sesame oil

Nutritional information:
Calories: 250 | Protein: 12g | Carbs: 18g | Fat: 14g | Fiber: 4g

Stuffed Bell Peppers with Lentils and Quinoa

Serves: 04
Prep. 15 mins
Easy
Cooking: 40 mins

COOKING STEPS

1. Preheat oven to 375°F (190°C). Place halved bell peppers on a baking sheet.
2. In a bowl, mix quinoa, lentils, diced tomatoes, paprika, cumin, salt, and pepper.
3. Stuff the mixture into the peppers and top with cheese if desired.
4. Bake for 30–35 minutes until peppers are tender.

INGREDIENTS

4 large bell peppers, halved and seeded
1 cup cooked quinoa
1 cup cooked lentils
1/2 cup diced tomatoes
1/4 cup shredded cheese (optional)
1 tsp smoked paprika
1 tsp cumin
Salt and pepper to taste

Nutritional information:
Calories: 210 | Protein: 10g | Carbs: 30g | Fat: 5g | Fiber: 8g

7.

Chickpea and Spinach Coconut Curry

Serves: 04 | Prep. 10 mins | Easy | Cooking: 20 mins

COOKING STEPS

1. Heat olive oil in a skillet and sauté garlic until fragrant.
2. Add tomatoes, curry powder, and turmeric. Cook for 2–3 minutes.
3. Stir in chickpeas, coconut milk, and spinach. Simmer for 10–15 minutes.
4. Serve over brown rice or quinoa.

INGREDIENTS

1 can (15 oz) chickpeas, rinsed and drained
2 cups fresh spinach
1 cup light coconut milk
1/2 cup diced tomatoes
2 cloves garlic, minced
1 tsp curry powder
1/2 tsp turmeric
1 tbsp olive oil

Nutritional information:
Calories: 280 | Protein: 9g | Carbs: 30g | Fat: 12g | Fiber: 7g

Turkey and Veggie Meatloaf

Serves: 06
Prep. 15 mins
Easy
Cooking: 50 mins

COOKING STEPS

1. Preheat oven to 375°F (190°C). Grease a loaf pan.
2. Mix all ingredients in a large bowl until well combined.
3. Press the mixture into the loaf pan and spread a thin layer of ketchup on top.
4. Bake for 45–50 minutes. Let cool for 5 minutes before slicing.

INGREDIENTS

1 lb ground turkey
1/2 cup grated zucchini
1/2 cup grated carrots
1/4 cup oats
1 egg
2 tbsp ketchup
1 tsp Worcestershire sauce
1/2 tsp garlic powder
Salt and pepper to taste

Nutritional information:
Calories: 220 | Protein: 18g | Carbs: 12g | Fat: 10g | Fiber: 2g

Baked Salmon with Veggie-Loaded Pesto

Serves: 04 | Prep. 10 mins | Easy | Cooking: 20 mins

COOKING STEPS

1. Preheat oven to 375°F (190°C). Place salmon fillets on a baking sheet lined with parchment paper.
2. In a blender, combine spinach, basil, walnuts, olive oil, garlic, lemon juice, salt, and pepper. Blend until smooth.
3. Spread the pesto over each salmon fillet.
4. Bake for 15–20 minutes until the salmon flakes easily with a fork.

INGREDIENTS

4 salmon fillets (4–6 oz each)
2 cups fresh spinach
1/2 cup fresh basil
1/4 cup walnuts
2 tbsp olive oil
1 clove garlic
Juice of 1 lemon
Salt and pepper to taste

Nutritional information:
Calories: 310 | Protein: 28g | Carbs: 4g | Fat: 20g | Fiber: 2g

CHAPTER 5
Snacks and Treats Made Healthy

Black Bean Brownies

Serves: 012
Prep. 10 mins
Easy
Cooking: 20 mins

COOKING STEPS

1. Preheat the oven to 350°F (175°C). Grease or line an 8x8-inch baking pan with parchment paper.
2. Blend black beans, eggs, coconut oil, cocoa powder, maple syrup, vanilla, baking powder, and salt in a food processor until smooth.
3. Fold in chocolate chips if desired. Pour batter into the prepared pan.
4. Bake for 18–20 minutes until set. Let cool before slicing.

TIP: For added flavor, sprinkle sea salt on top before baking.

INGREDIENTS

1 can (15 oz) black beans, rinsed and drained
3 large eggs
1/3 cup coconut oil, melted
1/2 cup cocoa powder
2/3 cup maple syrup
1 tsp vanilla extract
1/2 tsp baking powder
Pinch of salt
Optional: 1/4 cup dark chocolate chips

Nutritional information:
Calories: 120 | Protein: 4g | Carbs: 18g | Fat: 5g | Fiber: 3g

Spinach Banana Smoothie

Serves: 02 | Prep. 5 mins | Easy | Cooking: 0 mins

COOKING STEPS

1. Combine all ingredients in a blender and blend until smooth.
2. Pour into glasses and enjoy immediately.

TIP: Freeze the bananas beforehand for a thicker, creamier texture.

INGREDIENTS

2 ripe bananas
1 cup fresh spinach
1 cup unsweetened almond milk
1/2 cup Greek yogurt
1 tbsp chia seeds
1 tsp honey (optional)

Nutritional information:
Calories: 150 | Protein: 6g | Carbs: 25g | Fat: 3g | Fiber: 4g

Zucchini Muffins

Serves: 012　　Prep. 15 mins

Easy　　Cooking: 25 mins

COOKING STEPS

1. Preheat the oven to 350°F (175°C). Line a muffin tin with paper liners.
2. In a large bowl, mix zucchini, honey, coconut oil, applesauce, and vanilla.
3. Stir in the flours, cinnamon, baking soda, and salt until just combined.
4. Divide the batter evenly among the muffin cups. Bake for 20–25 minutes or until a toothpick comes out clean.

TIP: Add a sprinkle of walnuts or dark chocolate chips for variety.

INGREDIENTS

1 1/2 cups grated zucchini
1/2 cup whole wheat flour
1/2 cup almond flour
1/3 cup honey
1/4 cup coconut oil, melted
1/2 cup unsweetened applesauce
1 tsp vanilla extract
1/2 tsp cinnamon
1/2 tsp baking soda
1/4 tsp salt

Nutritional information:
Calories: 110 | Protein: 3g | Carbs: 18g | Fat: 4g | Fiber: 2g

Avocado Chocolate Mousse

Serves: 04 | Prep. 5 mins | Easy | Cooking: 0 mins

COOKING STEPS

1. Scoop the avocado flesh into a blender or food processor.
2. Add cocoa powder, maple syrup, vanilla, and salt. Blend until creamy and smooth.
3. Divide into small bowls or ramekins and chill for at least 30 minutes before serving.

TIP: Top with fresh berries or a dollop of Greek yogurt for a decorative touch.

INGREDIENTS

2 ripe avocados
1/3 cup cocoa powder
1/3 cup maple syrup
1/2 tsp vanilla extract
Pinch of salt

Nutritional information:
Calories: 210 | Protein: 3g | Carbs: 20g | Fat: 15g | Fiber: 7g

Carrot Cake Energy Balls

Serves: 012 | Prep. 10 mins | Easy | Cooking: 0 mins

COOKING STEPS

1. Combine all ingredients in a food processor. Pulse until the mixture forms a sticky dough.
2. Roll into bite-sized balls and refrigerate for at least 20 minutes before serving.

TIP: Store in an airtight container for up to a week for an easy grab-and-go snack.

INGREDIENTS

1 cup shredded carrots
1 cup rolled oats
1/4 cup almond butter
1/4 cup raisins
2 tbsp chia seeds
2 tbsp maple syrup
1/2 tsp cinnamon
1/4 tsp nutmeg

Nutritional information:
Calories: 80 | Protein: 2g | Carbs: 12g | Fat: 3g | Fiber: 2g

Sweet Potato Chocolate Chip Cookies

Serves: 18 cookies

Prep. 15 mins

Easy

Cooking: 12 mins

COOKING STEPS

1. Preheat oven to 350°F (175°C). Line a baking sheet with parchment paper.
2. In a large bowl, combine mashed sweet potato, almond butter, and coconut sugar until smooth.
3. Add oat flour, cinnamon, and baking soda, mixing until just combined. Fold in chocolate chips.
4. Scoop dough onto the baking sheet. Flatten slightly.
5. Bake for 10–12 minutes. Cool before serving.

INGREDIENTS

1 cup mashed sweet potato
1/2 cup almond butter
1/3 cup coconut sugar
1 cup oat flour
1 tsp cinnamon
1/2 tsp baking soda
1/3 cup dark chocolate chips

Nutritional information:
Calories: 90 | Protein: 2g | Carbs: 12g | Fat: 4g | Fiber: 2g

Hidden Veggie Pita Chips with Hummus

Serves: 04
Prep. 10 mins
Easy
Cooking: 15 mins

Cooking Steps

1. Preheat oven to 375°F (190°C). Slice pita breads into triangles.
2. Toss with olive oil, garlic powder, and smoked paprika. Spread on a baking sheet.
3. Bake for 10–15 minutes until crisp.
4. Blend baby spinach into hummus and serve with pita chips.

Ingredients

4 whole-grain pita breads
2 tbsp olive oil
1/2 tsp garlic powder
1/2 tsp smoked paprika
1/2 cup baby spinach (blended into hummus)
1 cup hummus

Nutritional information:
Calories: 180 | Protein: 5g | Carbs: 22g | Fat: 7g | Fiber: 5g

Beet and Berry Smoothie Popsicles

Serves: 8 popsicles
Prep. 10 mins
Easy
Cooking: 5 mins

COOKING STEPS

1. Blend all ingredients until smooth.
2. Pour into popsicle molds and freeze for at least 4 hours.

TIP: For a tangy twist, add a squeeze of lemon juice.

INGREDIENTS

1 cup cooked beets, chopped
1 1/2 cups mixed berries (e.g., strawberries, blueberries)
1 cup unsweetened almond milk
1/4 cup Greek yogurt
2 tbsp honey

Nutritional information:
Calories: 50 | Protein: 2g | Carbs: 9g | Fat: 1g | Fiber: 2g

Chickpea Blondies

Serves: 012 | Prep. 10 mins | Easy | Cooking: 25 mins

COOKING STEPS

1. Preheat oven to 350°F (175°C). Line an 8x8-inch pan with parchment paper.
2. Blend chickpeas, almond butter, maple syrup, vanilla, and baking powder until smooth.
3. Stir in chocolate chips and spread into the pan.
4. Bake for 20–25 minutes. Cool before slicing.

INGREDIENTS

1 can (15 oz) chickpeas, drained and rinsed
1/3 cup almond butter
1/4 cup maple syrup
1/2 tsp vanilla extract
1/4 tsp baking powder
1/4 cup dark chocolate chips

Nutritional information:
Calories: 100 | Protein: 3g | Carbs: 13g | Fat: 4g | Fiber: 2g

Apple Nachos with Nut Butter Drizzle

Serves: 02 | Prep. 5 mins | Easy | Cooking: 0 mins

Cooking Steps

1. Arrange apple slices on a plate.
2. Warm almond butter and honey slightly, then drizzle over apples.
3. Sprinkle with chia seeds and shredded coconut.

Ingredients

1 large apple, thinly sliced
2 tbsp almond or peanut butter
1 tsp honey
1 tbsp chia seeds
1 tbsp shredded coconut

Nutritional information:

Calories: 150 | Protein: 3g | Carbs: 22g | Fat: 7g | Fiber: 4g

PART 3: ADVANCED MEAL PREP STRATEGIES

Stealth Health Cookbook

CHAPTER 6

Customizing Meal Prep for Specific Needs

Meal prepping can be a lifesaver, but it becomes even more powerful when tailored to specific dietary needs. By making thoughtful substitutions, you can maintain balance, flavor, and nutrition while aligning with plant-based, keto, paleo, or gluten-free requirements. Let's explore how to customize meal prep for these diets effectively.

Plant-Based and Vegan-Friendly Options

Creating plant-based meal prep dishes involves replacing animal products with plant-derived alternatives while ensuring nutrient adequacy.

Key Tips:

- **Protein Boosters:** Use legumes, tofu, tempeh, seitan, edamame, lentils, and chickpeas to meet protein needs.

- **Dairy Replacements:** Opt for unsweetened almond milk, oat milk, or coconut milk. Use nutritional yeast as a cheesy flavor substitute.

- **Egg Alternatives:** Replace eggs with flaxseed meal (1 tbsp flaxseed + 3 tbsp water = 1 egg) or aquafaba (chickpea water).

- **Hidden Veggies:** Incorporate shredded zucchini, carrots, or cauliflower rice into dishes for added fiber and nutrients.

Recipe Example:

Vegan Chickpea Buddha Bowl

- **Base:** Quinoa or brown rice.

- **Protein:** Spiced roasted chickpeas.

- **Veggies:** Steamed broccoli, roasted sweet potatoes, shredded red cabbage.

- **Dressing:** Tahini mixed with lemon juice, garlic, and water for consistency.

- **Make-Ahead Tip:** Store components separately to keep them fresh.

Keto, Paleo, and Low-Carb Strategies

These diets focus on limiting carbs and prioritizing healthy fats and protein.

Key Tips:

- **Low-Carb Staples:** Use cauliflower rice, zucchini noodles, and spaghetti squash instead of grains and pasta.

- **Healthy Fats:** Incorporate avocado, nuts, seeds, olive oil, and coconut oil.

- **Protein Sources:** Stick to grass-fed meats, eggs, and fatty fish like salmon.

- **Flavor Enhancers:** Herbs and spices can mimic the umami taste often derived from sugar or starch-heavy bases.

Recipe Example:

Creamy Zucchini Noodle Alfredo (Keto & Paleo)

- **Base:** Spiralized zucchini noodles.

- **Sauce:** Blend cashews soaked in water, garlic, and nutritional yeast for a creamy texture.

- **Protein:** Add grilled chicken or shrimp.

- **Make-Ahead Tip:** Store sauce and noodles separately to prevent sogginess.

Gluten-Free and Allergy-Safe Meal Prep

For those avoiding gluten or allergens, focus on naturally gluten-free whole foods and check for hidden sources of allergens in condiments and prepackaged items.

Key Tips:

- **Grain Alternatives:** Quinoa, buckwheat, and wild rice are excellent replacements for wheat-based grains.

- **Flour Substitutions:** Use almond flour, coconut flour, or chickpea flour for baking and thickening.

- **Allergen-Free Proteins:** Stick to fresh meats, tofu (check soy allergies), or legumes.

- **Hidden Nutrients:** Add puréed butternut squash or spinach into sauces for additional nutrients.

Recipe Example:

Gluten-Free Veggie & Turkey Meatballs

- **Protein:** Ground turkey combined with grated zucchini and almond flour.
- **Binding Agent:** Use a flax egg or gluten-free breadcrumbs.
- **Serving:** Pair with roasted spaghetti squash and marinara sauce.
- **Make-Ahead Tip:** Freeze uncooked meatballs for quick future use.

Pro Tips for All Diets:

- **Batch Cooking:** Cook large portions of grains, legumes, or proteins to mix and match throughout the week.
- **Portioning:** Use divided containers to keep meal components fresh and customizable.
- **Labeling:** Mark containers to prevent cross-contamination for gluten-free or allergen-safe meals.

By implementing these strategies and recipes, meal prep becomes a versatile and practical tool for maintaining a healthy lifestyle tailored to your needs. Let me know if you'd like more recipe examples or guidance!

CHAPTER 7

Boosting Nutrient Absorption Through Smart Pairings

Eating nutrient-rich foods is important, but knowing how to pair them can make a significant difference in how your body absorbs and uses these nutrients. By combining the right foods, you can amplify their health benefits, making your meals more effective in supporting overall well-being.

Combining Foods for Maximum Health Benefits

Certain nutrients work better when paired with others. These combinations improve bioavailability—the ability of your body to absorb and utilize nutrients effectively. Here's how:

- **Vitamin C + Iron**: Non-heme iron (from plant sources) is harder for the body to absorb, but pairing it with vitamin C boosts absorption significantly.
- **Healthy Fats + Fat-Soluble Vitamins**: Vitamins A, D, E, and K are fat-soluble, meaning they require dietary fat to be absorbed.
- **Calcium + Vitamin D**: Vitamin D helps your body absorb calcium, essential for strong bones and teeth.
- **Zinc + Sulfur Compounds**: Found in garlic and onion, sulfur compounds enhance zinc absorption, which supports immune health.
- **Turmeric + Black Pepper**: The compound curcumin in turmeric becomes far more bioavailable when paired with piperine in black pepper.

Examples of Perfect Nutritional Pairings

1. Spinach Salad with Citrus Dressing

Nutritional Goal: Boost iron absorption.

- **Why It Works:** Spinach is rich in non-heme iron, while citrus fruits provide vitamin C to enhance absorption.

- **Recipe:** Toss baby spinach with orange slices, cherry tomatoes, red onion, and a lemon vinaigrette made with olive oil for added fat-soluble vitamins.

2. Avocado Toast with Carrot and Red Pepper Slaw

Nutritional Goal: Absorb fat-soluble vitamins.

- **Why It Works:** Carrots and red peppers are loaded with vitamin A, which pairs perfectly with the healthy fats in avocado.
- **Recipe:** Top whole-grain toast with mashed avocado, grated carrot, and thinly sliced red bell pepper. Drizzle with olive oil for added richness.

3. Lentil Soup with a Squeeze of Lemon

Nutritional Goal: Enhance iron absorption.

- **Why It Works:** Lentils are high in iron, and lemon juice provides vitamin C for better absorption.
- **Recipe:** Cook lentils with garlic, onion, carrots, and tomatoes. Finish with a generous squeeze of fresh lemon juice before serving.

4. Salmon with a Side of Kale and Sweet Potato Mash

Nutritional Goal: Boost calcium absorption.

- **Why It Works:** Kale provides calcium, while salmon offers vitamin D, helping your body absorb the calcium more effectively.
- **Recipe:** Serve grilled salmon with steamed kale and mashed sweet potatoes for a nutrient-packed dinner.

5. Golden Turmeric Latte with Black Pepper

Nutritional Goal: Enhance curcumin bioavailability.

- **Why It Works:** Curcumin in turmeric is better absorbed when combined with black pepper.
- **Recipe:** Heat almond milk with turmeric, a pinch of black pepper, cinnamon, and a touch of honey. Whisk until frothy.

6. Garlic-Infused Quinoa with Pumpkin Seeds

Nutritional Goal: Absorb more zinc.

- **Why It Works:** Sulfur compounds in garlic enhance zinc absorption from pumpkin seeds.

- **Recipe:** Cook quinoa with minced garlic and vegetable broth. Stir in toasted pumpkin seeds and chopped parsley for garnish.

Pro Tips for Maximum Nutritional Benefits

- **Eat Fresh:** Some nutrients, like vitamin C, are sensitive to heat. Add them towards the end of cooking.

- **Balance Variety:** Eating diverse foods ensures you get complementary nutrients.

- **Mind the Timing:** Pairing matters most during digestion, so combine these foods in the same meal for best results.

Incorporating these pairings into your meals not only makes them more flavorful but also unlocks their full nutritional potential. Let your meals work harder for your health!

CHAPTER 8

Streamlining Prep for Busy Lifestyles

When life is fast-paced, preparing healthy meals can feel like a challenge. However, with smart strategies like freezer hacks, batch cooking, and rotating seasonal ingredients, you can ensure that wholesome meals are always within reach. These techniques not only save time but also reduce waste and bring variety to your table.

Time-Saving Freezer and Fridge Hacks

1. **Pre-Chop and Freeze Vegetables**
   - **What to Do:** Chop onions, bell peppers, carrots, and celery in bulk and store them in freezer-safe bags.
   - **Why It Works:** Frozen pre-chopped veggies make soups, stir-fries, and casseroles come together in minutes.
   - **Pro Tip:** Blanch tougher vegetables like broccoli or green beans before freezing to preserve their texture.

2. **Portion Out Protein**
   - **What to Do:** Divide chicken, fish, or ground meat into meal-sized portions before freezing.
   - **Why It Works:** Smaller portions thaw faster and reduce the need to defrost an entire pack when you only need a little.
   - **Cooking Tip:** Marinate proteins before freezing to infuse flavor and skip a prep step later.

3. **Double Batch, Freeze Half**
   - **What to Do:** When making soups, stews, or casseroles, prepare a double batch and freeze half in portioned containers.
   - **Why It Works:** You'll always have a homemade meal ready when life gets hectic.

- **Example:** Freeze chili, lasagna, or vegetable curry in single servings for easy lunches or dinners.

4. **Freeze Smoothie Packs**
   - **What to Do:** Pre-portion fruits, spinach, and seeds into freezer bags for smoothies.
   - **Why It Works:** All you need is to add liquid and blend for a quick, nutrient-packed breakfast.
   - **Best Combos:** Banana, spinach, and mango; or blueberries, kale, and almond butter.

5. **Fridge Zone Organization**
   - **What to Do:** Use clear containers to organize prepped ingredients in your fridge.
   - **Why It Works:** Prepped produce, cooked grains, and proteins are easy to grab, minimizing midweek chaos.
   - **Example:** Store cooked quinoa, roasted vegetables, and boiled eggs in labeled sections.

Rotating Recipes and Seasonal Ingredients

1. **Base Ingredients, Multiple Recipes**
   - **Example:** Cook a batch of quinoa and use it in multiple dishes:
     - **Day 1:** Quinoa salad with roasted vegetables.
     - **Day 2:** Quinoa-stuffed bell peppers.
     - **Day 3:** Quinoa breakfast bowl with almond milk and fruit.

2. **Focus on Seasonal Produce**
   - **Why It Works:** Seasonal ingredients are fresher, more flavorful, and often more affordable.
   - **Example:** In summer, rotate through dishes featuring tomatoes, zucchini, and peaches. In winter, focus on hearty options with squash, kale, and citrus.

3. **Flavor Variations for Similar Bases**
    - **Strategy:** Prepare one base recipe and alter the seasonings or toppings.
    - **Example:**
        - **Base:** Roasted chicken thighs.
        - **Variation 1:** Serve with pesto and roasted veggies.
        - **Variation 2:** Shred and toss into tacos with lime crema.
        - **Variation 3:** Use in a comforting chicken soup with herbs.
4. **Batch Cook Grains and Legumes**
    - **What to Do:** Cook large batches of rice, farro, or lentils to use in various meals.
    - **Why It Works:** Pre-cooked staples allow for quick assembly of grain bowls, soups, and side dishes.
    - **Example:** Add lentils to a salad one day and use them for a curry the next.
5. **Plan Around Versatile Sauces**
    - **Example:** Make a batch of tahini dressing, chimichurri, or peanut sauce to use across several meals.
    - **Why It Works:** A flavorful sauce can transform a simple dish into something special without extra effort.

Putting It All Together: A Meal Prep Example

Weeknight Burrito Bowls

- **Prep Ahead:**
    - Cook a large batch of brown rice and black beans.
    - Chop and freeze peppers and onions.
    - Make a jar of homemade salsa or guacamole.
- **Assembly:**

- Warm the rice and beans, sauté frozen peppers and onions, and top with salsa, guacamole, and shredded cheese.
- Serve with lime wedges for brightness.

PART 4: SUSTAINING YOUR STEALTH HEALTH JOURNEY

CHAPTER 9

Creating a Sustainable Meal Prep Routine

A sustainable meal prep routine isn't just about saving time—it's about building a system that keeps you consistent while reducing stress, food waste, and overspending. By following weekly templates and embracing budget-friendly strategies, you can create a long-term routine that works for you, no matter your lifestyle.

Weekly Templates for Meal Planning

1. **Define Your Weekly Menu Structure**

Example Template:

1. **Monday:** Meatless meal (e.g., veggie stir-fry)
2. **Tuesday:** Protein-packed bowl (e.g., chicken and quinoa)
3. **Wednesday:** Slow cooker dish (e.g., chili)
4. **Thursday:** Leftovers or mix-and-match
5. **Friday:** Treat meal (e.g., homemade pizza)

Why It Works: It provides variety while keeping your planning focused.

2. **Plan for Versatile Ingredients**

    - Choose items like roasted vegetables, grains, or cooked proteins that can be used in multiple dishes throughout the week.

    - **Example:** Roast a batch of sweet potatoes to use in salads, tacos, and breakfast hash.

3. **Time Block for Prep**

    - Dedicate one or two sessions each week for meal prep.

    - **Tip:** Break it into stages: chopping vegetables, cooking grains, and portioning proteins.

4. **Prep for Snacks and Breakfasts**

- o Don't forget smaller meals! Prep smoothie packs, overnight oats, or homemade energy bars to stay fueled throughout the day.

5. **Keep a Meal Prep Calendar**
    - o Use a whiteboard or an app to outline meals for the week.
    - o **Why It's Helpful:** It gives you a visual guide to stay organized and avoid last-minute decisions.

SCAN THE CODE BELOW FOR A FREE DASH DIET MEAL PREP PLAN

Budget-Friendly Meal Prep Tips

1. **Buy in Bulk**
    - Shop for grains, legumes, and pantry staples in bulk to reduce costs.
    - **Pro Tip:** Use bulk purchases for batch cooking items like rice, beans, or pasta.

2. **Plan Around Sales and Seasonal Produce**
    - Check your local grocery store's sales flyer before planning meals.
    - **Example:** Use zucchini or tomatoes in summer and squash or kale in winter.

3. **Embrace Simple Ingredients**
    - You don't need exotic items to make delicious meals. Stick to affordable basics like eggs, potatoes, carrots, and canned beans.
    - **Cooking Tip:** Spices and herbs can transform any simple dish into something exciting.

4. **Repurpose Leftovers**
    - Use roasted chicken for dinner, and repurpose it into chicken salad wraps for lunch the next day.
    - **Smart Example:** Turn leftover quinoa into breakfast porridge by adding almond milk, cinnamon, and berries.

5. **Batch Cook and Freeze**
    - Make large portions of soups, stews, or casseroles and freeze them in individual servings.
    - **Why It Works:** It's like having your own lineup of ready-made meals without paying for takeout.

Strategies for Staying Consistent

1. **Keep Your Pantry Stocked**
    - Maintain a list of essentials like olive oil, garlic, onions, and spices. A stocked pantry makes improvisation easy.

2. **Simplify with Repeated Meals**
   - It's okay to have the same lunch or dinner a few times a week. Focus on recipes you enjoy and rotate them periodically.

3. **Use Time-Saving Tools**
   - Invest in a slow cooker, pressure cooker, or food processor to streamline prep and cooking.

4. **Involve the Whole Family**
   - Assign meal prep tasks to family members, such as chopping, stirring, or organizing ingredients.

5. **Evaluate and Adjust**
   - Reflect on what worked and what didn't each week, and make small adjustments. This iterative process builds long-term habits.

CHAPTER 10

Overcoming Common Challenges

Meal prep offers many benefits, but it's not without its hurdles. From picky eaters who refuse certain foods to the creeping monotony of repetitive meals, these challenges can make meal planning feel daunting. Let's tackle these obstacles with actionable strategies to keep your meal prep vibrant, adaptable, and enjoyable.

Handling Picky Eaters with Stealth Health Tricks

Whether you're cooking for children or adults with selective tastes, stealth health techniques can make meals both nutritious and appealing without drawing attention to the "hidden" ingredients.

1. Blend and Hide

- **Smoothies:** Add a handful of spinach or kale to fruit-based smoothies. The vibrant flavors of mango, pineapple, or berries mask the greens completely.
- **Soups:** Puree vegetables like carrots, zucchini, or cauliflower into soups for a creamy texture without the need for cream.

2. Sneak in Grains and Veggies

- **Rice Substitutes:** Use cauliflower rice or mix in quinoa with white rice.
- **Mac and Cheese Upgrade:** Blend cooked butternut squash or sweet potato into the cheese sauce.

3. Involve Them in Cooking

- Let picky eaters help assemble meals, such as build-your-own tacos or pizza. Offer a variety of toppings, including hidden healthy options like finely diced veggies.

4. Make Familiar Foods Healthier

- **Burgers:** Use ground turkey or chicken with grated zucchini for extra moisture and nutrients.

- **Chicken Nuggets:** Coat chicken strips in crushed whole-grain cereal or almond flour before baking.

Preventing Burnout and Keeping Prep Exciting

Even the most dedicated meal preppers can hit a wall when faced with endless chopping or eating the same meals on repeat. Here's how to inject creativity and ease into the process.

1. Rotate Flavors

- Explore different cuisines each week—think Mexican-inspired bowls one week, Mediterranean wraps the next.
- Use spice blends or sauces like harissa, chimichurri, or tahini to transform basic proteins and vegetables.

2. Batch Prep Core Ingredients

- Prep versatile ingredients like roasted vegetables, grains, or shredded chicken that can be used in various recipes.
- **Example:** Use roasted sweet potatoes in a breakfast hash, lunchtime salad, and dinner grain bowl.

3. Embrace Freezer-Friendly Meals

- Prepare meals that can be frozen in individual portions, such as lasagna, soups, or stuffed peppers. Rotate these meals weekly to keep things fresh.

4. Incorporate New Recipes Regularly

- Commit to trying one new recipe a week to keep your culinary skills sharp and your taste buds engaged.
- Join meal prep groups or browse online forums for inspiration and trends.

5. Take Breaks When Needed

- Use shortcuts like pre-chopped vegetables, store-bought rotisserie chicken, or meal delivery kits when life gets hectic. These tools keep you consistent without overextending yourself.

Real-Life Examples

- **Family Scenario:** A mom of two picky eaters preps chicken and veggie quesadillas, using finely grated zucchini in the cheese filling. Her kids love the crispy texture and have no idea they're eating veggies.

- **Busy Professional:** A single professional combats burnout by freezing portions of lentil soup, turkey chili, and stir-fried rice. Each week, they rotate meals to keep things interesting.

- **Fitness Enthusiast:** A health-conscious individual preps smoothie packs with spinach, frozen berries, and protein powder. In the mornings, they just add almond milk and blend.

By tailoring strategies to your lifestyle and preferences, you can overcome common meal prep challenges with ease, ensuring your routine stays both efficient and enjoyable.

CHAPTER 11

Celebrating Progress

Meal prepping is more than just a practical way to save time; it's a lifestyle shift that can transform your health, energy levels, and relationship with food. By embracing stealth health principles—making meals nutritious without sacrificing flavor—you can enjoy lasting benefits while inspiring others to take control of their well-being.

How Meal Prep Transforms Your Health

1. Elevated Energy Levels

Imagine starting your day with a nutrient-packed breakfast and continuing with balanced, pre-prepared meals. When you fuel your body consistently, you experience fewer energy crashes, better focus, and improved stamina.

- **Example:** A working mom swaps processed snacks for prepped veggie sticks with hummus and quinoa bowls for lunch. She notices she's no longer relying on coffee in the afternoon to stay alert.

2. Improved Physical Health

Strategic meal prep can lead to weight management, reduced inflammation, and lower risk of chronic diseases. Incorporating stealth health techniques like veggie-rich casseroles or protein-packed desserts ensures you're meeting your nutritional needs.

- **Example:** A man with high cholesterol starts meal prepping salmon with roasted Brussels sprouts and sweet potatoes. Within three months, his cholesterol levels improve significantly, impressing his doctor.

3. Confidence in Cooking

Learning to meal prep boosts your cooking skills and creativity. By trying new ingredients and techniques, you become more comfortable experimenting in the kitchen.

- **Example:** A college student transitions from ramen noodles to prepping healthy stir-fry meals. Their confidence grows, and they eventually start cooking for friends, spreading the healthful habits.

Stories of Success and Inspiration

The Transformation of Lisa: A Busy Professional

Lisa, a marketing executive, was always exhausted by midday, surviving on vending machine snacks and takeout dinners. Determined to make a change, she started prepping overnight oats for breakfast, grilled chicken salads for lunch, and hearty vegetable soups for dinner.

- **Result:** Within six weeks, Lisa felt more energized, lost 10 pounds, and noticed clearer skin. She inspired her coworkers to start a meal-prep challenge, creating a ripple effect of health in her office.

James' Journey to Control Diabetes

James was diagnosed with Type 2 diabetes and overwhelmed by dietary restrictions. He began prepping meals tailored to his needs, using stealth health hacks like replacing pasta with zucchini noodles and swapping sugary desserts for avocado-based chocolate mousse.

- **Result:** After three months, James' blood sugar levels stabilized, and his doctor reduced his medication dosage. His success motivated him to share recipes with a local diabetes support group.

Maria's Family Transformation

As a mother of three picky eaters, Maria struggled to get her kids to eat vegetables. She started incorporating hidden ingredients into their favorite dishes, like blending spinach into marinara sauce and adding shredded zucchini to meatballs.

- **Result:** Her kids began eating balanced meals without complaints, and Maria's husband joined in, losing 15 pounds and feeling more energetic at work.

The Tangible Benefits of Meal Prep

- **Better Mood and Mental Clarity:** Balanced meals with whole foods stabilize blood sugar levels, improving mood and focus.

- **Weight Management:** Controlling portions and reducing reliance on processed foods aids in achieving fitness goals.
- **Less Food Waste:** Pre-planned meals use up ingredients efficiently, saving money and resources.

Meal prep isn't just about the food you eat—it's about taking control of your life. By setting aside time to prepare nourishing meals, you're investing in your health and creating a ripple effect of positive change. Whether you're transforming your own habits or inspiring those around you, every step forward is worth celebrating.

Conclusion

Embarking on the journey to healthier eating doesn't have to be daunting. With stealth health strategies and meal prep techniques, you can transform the way you nourish your body and enjoy food. Small changes, like sneaking extra vegetables into a favorite dish or planning meals ahead of time, create a ripple effect that leads to big improvements in energy, health, and overall well-being.

Why Stealth Health Works

Stealth health is about subtle, impactful choices that prioritize nutrition without compromising taste. By focusing on nutrient-dense swaps—such as cauliflower rice for traditional grains or black beans in brownies—you can enjoy the flavors you love while fueling your body with essential vitamins and minerals. These strategies make it easier to adopt healthy habits that stick.

The Benefits of Starting Now

- **Convenience:** Meal prepping simplifies busy days. Having ready-to-eat meals saves time and reduces stress.

- **Balanced Nutrition:** Thoughtfully prepared meals ensure you're getting the nutrients your body needs to thrive.

- **Improved Energy and Focus:** Wholesome meals stabilize blood sugar levels, keeping you energized throughout the day.

- **Confidence in the Kitchen:** Experimenting with recipes fosters creativity and makes cooking more enjoyable.

How to Get Started

1. **Start Small:** Choose one or two recipes to prep each week. Experiment with simple stealth health techniques, like adding finely chopped vegetables to casseroles or blending greens into smoothies.

2. **Plan Ahead:** Use the templates and meal prep strategies provided in this guide. Build a grocery list that aligns with your health goals and keeps things manageable.

3. **Celebrate Progress:** Each step forward, no matter how small, brings you closer to a healthier lifestyle. Enjoy the process and reflect on the positive changes you're experiencing.

A Healthier You, One Bite at a Time

The tools, tips, and recipes in this guide are your roadmap to a sustainable, nourishing, and delicious lifestyle. Whether you're meal prepping for a busy week, sneaking more nutrients into family meals, or exploring new flavors, every effort you make is an investment in yourself.

The path to a healthier, tastier life is within reach. Take that first step today—your future self will thank you.

Appendices

Pantry Staples for Stealth Health Success

Building a stealth health pantry is key to making nutritious, flavorful meals at any time. These staples are versatile, nutrient-rich, and perfect for sneaking healthy ingredients into dishes.

- **Whole Grains:** Quinoa, brown rice, farro, and whole-grain pasta are fiber-packed alternatives that enhance satiety and support digestion.

- **Legumes:** Keep canned or dried lentils, chickpeas, and black beans handy. They're excellent protein and fiber sources, ideal for soups, stews, and even desserts.

- **Healthy Oils and Fats:** Stock olive oil, avocado oil, and nut butters. These heart-healthy fats enhance flavor and support brain health.

- **Nutritional Yeast:** A plant-based favorite that adds a cheesy flavor while delivering a boost of B vitamins.

- **Flour Alternatives:** Almond flour, oat flour, and coconut flour work for gluten-free baking or breading, adding unique flavors and nutrients.

- **Shelf-Stable Vegetables:** Canned tomatoes, tomato paste, and jarred roasted peppers provide convenience and rich flavors for countless recipes.

- **Spices and Herbs:** Include turmeric, cumin, cinnamon, paprika, and dried basil. Spices enhance flavor without added sodium and contribute antioxidants.

- **Natural Sweeteners:** Use honey, maple syrup, or stevia for sweetness without refined sugar spikes.

Meal Prep Shopping Lists by Recipe

To streamline meal prep, pre-organized shopping lists make a big difference. Below are examples of lists tailored to recipes:

Recipe: Spinach and Chickpea Curry

- Fresh Produce: Spinach (4 cups), onion (1 large), garlic (4 cloves), ginger (1-inch piece).

- Pantry: Chickpeas (2 cans), canned tomatoes (1 can), coconut milk (1 can).
- Spices: Turmeric, cumin, paprika, coriander.
- Staples: Olive oil, salt, and pepper.

Recipe: Black Bean Brownies

- Pantry: Black beans (1 can), cocoa powder, rolled oats, dark chocolate chips.
- Staples: Honey or maple syrup, vanilla extract.

Tips for Shopping Efficiency:

1. **Group by Section:** Organize the list by store sections (produce, pantry, dairy).
2. **Opt for Seasonal Ingredients:** Choose in-season produce to save money and maximize flavor.
3. **Check Stock First:** Inventory your pantry and freezer to avoid duplicates.

Quick Nutritional Reference Guide

Understanding basic nutrition helps you make informed choices. Here's a simple breakdown:

- **Macronutrients:**
    - **Carbohydrates:** The body's primary energy source. Focus on whole grains, fruits, and vegetables.
    - **Proteins:** Crucial for muscle repair and overall health. Incorporate plant-based sources like beans, tofu, and nuts.
    - **Fats:** Support brain function and hormone production. Choose healthy fats like those in avocado, olive oil, and seeds.
- **Vitamins:**
    - **Vitamin C:** Boosts immunity and aids iron absorption. Found in citrus fruits, bell peppers, and broccoli.
    - **Vitamin D:** Supports bone health. Look for fortified foods or get sunlight exposure.
    - **B Vitamins:** Vital for energy production and brain health. Found in whole grains, eggs, and leafy greens.
- **Minerals:**
    - **Iron:** Essential for oxygen transport in the blood. Pair plant-based sources like spinach with vitamin C-rich foods for better absorption.
    - **Calcium:** Builds strong bones and teeth. Found in dairy and fortified plant-based milk.
    - **Magnesium:** Supports muscle and nerve function. Found in nuts, seeds, and legumes.

By integrating these tools into your routine, you're equipped to create meals that are not just delicious but also nutritious and efficient. With a well-stocked pantry, organized shopping lists, and an understanding of nutrition, healthy eating becomes a natural part of your daily life.

BONUS SECTION

BONUS 1 GLOSSARY TEMPLATE

Grocery LIST

Vegetables:	Fruits:	Meat and Poultry:
○ ○ ○ ○ ○ ○ ○	○ ○ ○ ○ ○ ○ ○	○ ○ ○ ○ ○ ○ ○

Seafood:	Dairy and Eggs:	Grains and Breads:
○ ○ ○ ○ ○ ○	○ ○ ○ ○ ○ ○	○ ○ ○ ○ ○ ○

Canned Goods:	Snacks and Treats:	Condiments:
○ ○ ○ ○ ○ ○	○ ○ ○ ○ ○ ○	○ ○ ○ ○ ○ ○

Miscellaneous Items:
○ ○ ○

Grocery LIST

Vegetables:	Fruits:	Meat and Poultry:
○ ○ ○ ○ ○ ○	○ ○ ○ ○ ○ ○	○ ○ ○ ○ ○ ○

Seafood:	Dairy and Eggs:	Grains and Breads:
○ ○ ○ ○ ○ ○	○ ○ ○ ○ ○ ○	○ ○ ○ ○ ○ ○

Canned Goods:	Snacks and Treats:	Condiments:
○ ○ ○ ○ ○ ○	○ ○ ○ ○ ○ ○	○ ○ ○ ○ ○ ○

Miscellaneous Items:

○
○
○

BONUS 2
Exclusive Meal Prep Tracker

MONDAY

___ / ___ / _____

TRACK TODAY

	BEFORE	AFTER
BREAKFAST		
LUNCH		
SNACK		
DINNER		

NOTE

MOOD:

TUESDAY

___ / ___ / _____

TRACK TODAY

	BEFORE	AFTER
BREAKFAST		
LUNCH		
SNACK		
DINNER		

NOTE

MOOD:

WEDNESDAY

__ / __ / ____

TRACK TODAY

	BEFORE	AFTER
BREAKFAST		
LUNCH		
SNACK		
DINNER		

NOTE:

MOOD:

THURSDAY

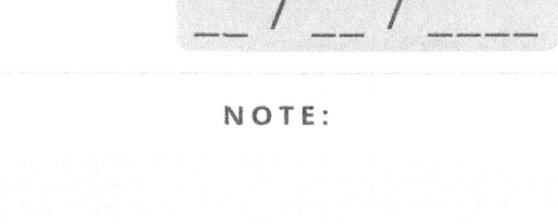

__ / __ / ____

TRACK TODAY

	BEFORE	AFTER
BREAKFAST		
LUNCH		
SNACK		
DINNER		

NOTE:

MOOD:

FRIDAY

___ / ___ / _____

TRACK TODAY

	BEFORE	AFTER
BREAKFAST		
LUNCH		
SNACK		
DINNER		

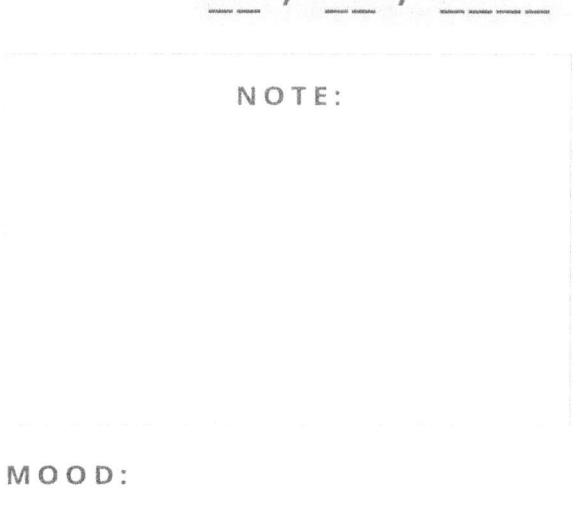

NOTE:

MOOD:

SATURDAY

___ / ___ / _____

TRACK TODAY

	BEFORE	AFTER
BREAKFAST		
LUNCH		
SNACK		
DINNER		

NOTE:

MOOD:

SUNDAY

__ / __ / ____

TRACK TODAY

	BEFORE	AFTER
BREAKFAST		
LUNCH		
SNACK		
DINNER		

NOTE:

MOOD:

WEEKLY SUMMARY

BONUS 3

DIY Spice Blends and Flavor Boosters

Creating your own spice blends and flavor enhancers is a simple way to elevate dishes while maintaining control over ingredients and nutritional content. Below is a guide presented in a clear and structured format for easy use.

Custom Spice Blends

BLEND NAME	INGREDIENTS	TIPS FOR USE
TACO SEASONING	2 tbsp chili powder, 1 tsp cumin, 1 tsp paprika, 1/2 tsp garlic powder, 1/2 tsp onion powder, 1/2 tsp oregano, 1/4 tsp cayenne pepper (optional), 1/2 tsp salt, 1/4 tsp black pepper	Sprinkle on ground beef, tofu, or roasted vegetables for tacos, fajitas, or burrito bowls.
MEDITERRANEAN HERB MIX	1 tbsp dried oregano, 1 tbsp thyme, 1 tsp rosemary, 1 tsp basil, 1/2 tsp garlic powder, 1/4 tsp salt	Use on roasted chicken, fish, or as a salad dressing base when combined with olive oil and lemon juice.
CURRY POWDER	2 tbsp turmeric, 1 tsp cumin, 1 tsp coriander, 1/2 tsp ginger powder, 1/4 tsp cinnamon, 1/4 tsp cardamom, pinch of cayenne pepper	Perfect for soups, stews, or as a seasoning for roasted chickpeas.

Flavor Boosters

ENHANCER	INGREDIENTS	PREPARATION TIPS
GARLIC HERB OIL	1 cup olive oil, 3 cloves garlic (smashed), 1 sprig rosemary, 1 tsp dried thyme	Heat oil on low, add garlic and herbs, simmer for 10 minutes. Strain and store in a glass bottle. Use for sautéing or drizzling.
CITRUS-CHILI DRESSING	Juice of 1 lime, 2 tbsp olive oil, 1/2 tsp chili flakes, pinch of salt	Shake in a jar and pour over salads, tacos, or grain bowls for a tangy-spicy kick.
LEMON-PEPPER SEASONING	2 tbsp dried lemon zest, 1 tbsp black pepper, 1 tsp garlic powder, 1/2 tsp onion powder	Sprinkle on fish, chicken, or steamed vegetables for a fresh burst of flavor.

Tips for Success

1. **Batch Preparation**: Double or triple recipes to store blends in airtight jars for future use. Label jars with the name and date for freshness.

2. **Customization**: Adjust salt and heat levels based on dietary preferences.

3. **Freshness Matters**: Use freshly ground spices whenever possible for maximum flavor.

4. **Creative Pairings**: Experiment with blends as dry rubs, marinades, or finishing touches on dishes.

These recipes not only save time but also ensure your meals are packed with flavor and tailored to your health goals.

BONUS 4

30-Minute Meal Prep Challenge

The **30-Minute Meal Prep Challenge** is designed to help you efficiently prepare a week's worth of meals in just half an hour. Follow this step-by-step guide to transform meal prep into a quick, effective, and fun experience.

WHAT YOU'LL ACCOMPLISH	WHAT YOU'LL NEED
Prep 3 meals for 5 days: Breakfast, Lunch, and Dinner.	Ingredients list (below), basic kitchen tools (knife, cutting board, containers, skillet, oven).

INGREDIENT LIST

CATEGORY	INGREDIENTS
PROTEINS	1 lb chicken breast (or tofu for a vegetarian option), 4 eggs, 1 can black beans.
VEGETABLES	2 bell peppers, 1 zucchini, 1 bag spinach, 1 sweet potato, cherry tomatoes.
GRAINS	2 cups quinoa or brown rice, 1 package whole-grain tortillas.
PANTRY STAPLES	Olive oil, salt, pepper, garlic powder, paprika, soy sauce, balsamic vinegar.

STEP-BY-STEP INSTRUCTIONS

TIME	TASK
0:00–5:00	Boil quinoa or rice and roast diced sweet potato in the oven (400°F, 15 minutes, olive oil, paprika).
5:00–10:00	Grill chicken breast or tofu with garlic powder and soy sauce in a skillet.
10:00–15:00	Scramble eggs and sauté spinach with olive oil.
15:00–20:00	Slice bell peppers and zucchini into strips for snacks or stir-fry later.
20:00–25:00	Assemble 3 wraps with tortillas: Add spinach, grilled chicken or tofu, and quinoa.
25:00–30:00	Portion roasted sweet potato and beans into containers with quinoa or rice for lunches.

FINAL CHECKLIST

☐ **Breakfast:** Spinach and egg scramble (prep ahead and reheat).

☐ **Lunch:** Sweet potato, black bean, and quinoa bowls.

☐ **Dinner:** Chicken or tofu wraps with fresh veggies.

☐ **Snacks:** Bell pepper and zucchini strips with hummus.

PRO TIPS

1. **Set a Timer**: Challenge yourself to stay on track for each task.

2. **Clean as You Go**: Minimize post-prep cleanup.

3. **Engage with the Community**: Share your creations on social media with a hashtag, like **#30MinuteMealPrep**, to inspire others.

This challenge is not only a time-saver but also a fun way to practice healthy eating habits. Get started today and see how easy it is to make meal prep a regular part of your lifestyle!

BONUS 5

conversion chart
FOR THE KITCHEN

VOLUME MEASUREMENT CONVERSIONS

Cups	Tablespoons	Teaspoons	Milliliters
1/16 cup	1 tbsp	1 tsp	5ml
1/8 cup	2 tbsp	3 tsp	15 ml
1/4 cup	4 tbsp	6 tsp	30 ml
1/3 cup	5 1/3 tbsp	12 tsp	60 ml
1/2 cup	8 tbsp	16 tsp	80 ml
2/3 cup	10 2/3 tbsp	24 tsp	120 ml
3/4 cup	12 tbsp	32 tsp	160 ml
1 cup	16 tbsp	36 tsp	180 ml
		48 tsp	240 ml

1 QUART =
2 pints
4 cups
32 ounces
950 ml

1 PINT =
2 cups
16 ounces
480 ml

1 CUP =
16 tbsp
8 ounces
240 ml

1/4 CUP =
4 tbsp
12 tsp
2 ounces
60 ml

1 TBSP =
3 tsp 1/2 ounce
15 ml

COOKING TEMPERATURE CONVERSIONS

Celcius/Centigrade F = (C × 1.8) + 32
Fahrenheit C = (F − 32) × 0.5556

BAKING INGREDIENT CONVERSIONS

BUTTER

Cups	Grams
1/4 cup	57 grams
1/3 cup	76 grams
1/2 cup	113 grams
1 cup	227 grams

PACKED BROWN SUGAR

Cups	Grams	Ounces
1/4 cup	55 grams	1.9 oz
1/3 cup	73 grams	2.58 oz
1/2 cup	110 grams	3.88 oz
1 cup	220 grams	7.75 oz

ALL-PURPOSE FLOUR / CONFECTIONER'S SUGAR

Cups	Grams	Ounces
1/8 cup	16 grams	563 oz
1/4 cup	32 grams	1.13 oz
1/3 cup	43 grams	1.5 oz
1/2 cup	64 grams	2.25 oz
2/3 cup	85 grams	3 oz
3/4 cup	96 grams	3.38 oz
1 cup	128 grams	4.5 oz

GRANULATED SUGAR

Cups	Grams	Ounces
2 tbsp	25 grams	89 oz
1/4 cup	67 grams	1.78 oz
1/3 cup	50 grams	2.37 oz
1/2 cup	100 grams	3.55 oz
2/3 cup	134 grams	4.73 oz
3/4 cup	150 grams	5.3 oz
1 cup	201 grams	7.1 oz

QUICK REFERENCE FOR MEASUREMENTS AND CONVERSIONS

VOLUME CONVERSIONS

US STANDARD	METRIC	UK IMPERIAL
1 teaspoon (tsp)	5 milliliters (ml)	1 UK teaspoon
1 tablespoon (tbsp)	15 milliliters (ml)	1 UK tablespoon
1 fluid ounce (fl oz)	30 milliliters (ml)	1 UK fluid ounce
1 cup	240 milliliters (ml)	1 UK cup (250 ml)
1 pint (pt)	480 milliliters (ml)	1 UK pint (568 ml)
1 quart (qt)	960 milliliters (ml)	1 UK quart (1.14 L)
1 gallon (gal)	3.8 liters (L)	1 UK gallon (4.55 L)

Made in the USA
Coppell, TX
13 May 2025